**STRUM IT GUITAR**

AUTHENTIC CHORDS
ORIGINAL KEYS
COMPLETE SONGS

IRVING BERLIN'S

# God Bless America®
## Songs of Inspiration

## ABOUT "GOD BLESS AMERICA"

"GOD BLESS AMERICA" by Irving Berlin was first published in 1938. Almost as soon as the song began generating revenue, Mr. Berlin established The God Bless America Fund to benefit American youth.

Over $6,000,000 has been distributed to date, primarily to two youth organizations with which Mr. and Mrs. Berlin were personally involved: the Girl Scout Council of Greater New York, and the Greater New York Councils of the Boy Scouts of America. These councils do not discriminate on any basis and are committed to serving all segments of New York City's diverse youth population.

The trustees of The God Bless America Fund are working with the two councils to ensure that funding is allocated for New York City children affected by the tragic events of September 11, 2001.

ISBN 0-634-04020-0

**HAL•LEONARD® CORPORATION**

7777 W. BLUEMOUND RD. P.O. BOX 13819 MILWAUKEE, WI 53213

Visit Hal Leonard Online at
**www.halleonard.com**

# HOW TO USE THIS BOOK

Strum It is the series designed especially to get you playing (and singing!) along with your favorite songs. The idea is simple—the songs are arranged using their original keys in lead sheet format, giving you the chords for each song, beginning to end. The melody and lyrics are also shown to help you keep your spot and sing along.

Rhythm slashes are written above the staff as an accompaniment suggestion. Strum the chords in the rhythm indicated. Use the chord diagrams found at the top of the first page of the arrangement for the appropriate chord voicings.

---

### Additional Musical Definitions

| | |
|---|---|
| ⊓ | • Downstroke |
| ∨ | • Upstroke |
| *D.S. al Coda* | • Go back to the sign (𝄋), then play until the measure marked *"To Coda,"* then skip to the section labelled *"Coda."* |
| *D.C. al Fine* | • Go back to the beginning of the song and play until the measure marked *"Fine"* (end). |
| *cont. rhy. sim.* | • Continue using similar rhythm pattern. |
| N.C. | • Instrument is silent (drops out). |
| 𝄆 𝄇 | • Repeat measures between signs. |
| 1. 2. | • When a repeated section has different endings, play the first ending only the first time and the second ending only the second time. |

# Contents

# Amazing Grace

**Words by John Newton**
**From A Collection of Sacred Ballads**
**Traditional American Melody**
**From Carrell and Clayton's Virginia Harmony**

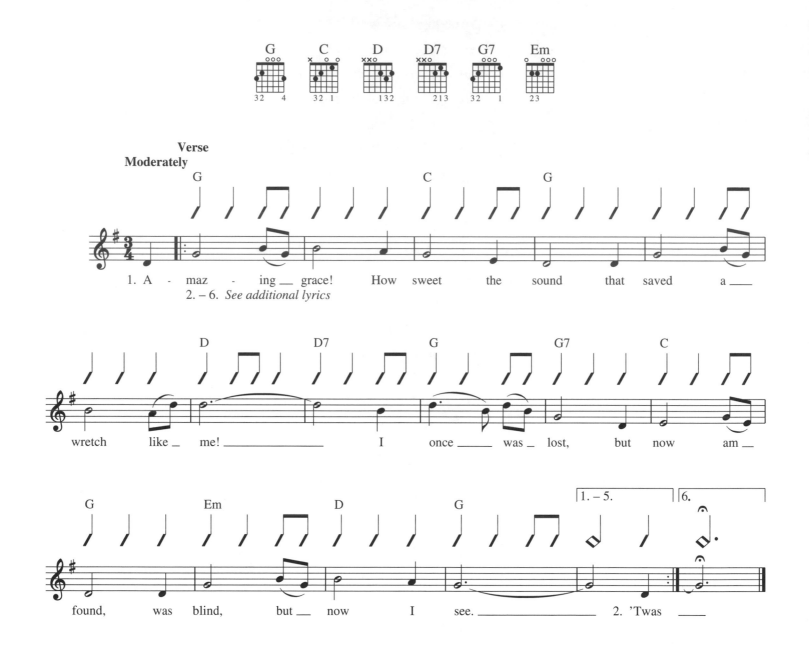

### Additional Lyrics

2. 'Twas grace that taught my heart to fear,
And grace my fears relieved.
How precious did that grace appear
The hour I first believed.

3. Through many dangers, toils and snares,
I have already come.
'Tis grace has brought me safe thus far,
And grace will lead me home.

4. The Lord has promised good to me,
His word my hope secures.
He will my shield and portion be
As long as life endures.

5. And when this flesh and heart shall fail,
And mortal life shall cease.
I shall posess within the veil
A life of joy and peace.

6. When we've been there ten thousand years,
Bright shining as the sun,
We've no less days to sing God's praise
Than when we first begun.

# America, the Beautiful

**Words by Katherine Lee Bates**
**Music by Samuel A. Ward**

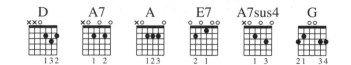

**Verse**
**Moderately slow**

1. O beau - ti - ful for spa - cious skies, for am - ber waves of grain, for
2. *See additional lyrics*

pur - ple moun - tain ma - jes - ties a - bove the fruit - ed plain. A -

mer - i - ca! A - mer - i - ca! God shed His grace on thee, and

crown thy good with broth - er-hood from sea to shin - ing sea. 2. O sea.

*Additional Lyrics*

2. O beautiful for patriot dream
That sees beyond the years,
Thine alabaster cities gleam
Undimmed by human tears.
America! America!
God shed His grace on thee,
And crown thy good with brotherhood
From sea to shining sea.

# Battle Hymn of the Republic

**Words by Julia Ward Howe**
**Music by William Steffe**

*Additional Lyrics*

2. I have seen Him in the watch-fires of a hundred circling camps,
   They have builded Him an altar in the evening dews and damps.
   I can read His righteous sentence by the dim and flaring lamps;
   His day is marching on.

3. He has sounded forth the trumpet that shall never sound retreat,
   He is sifting out the hearts of men before His judgment seat.
   O be swift, my soul, to answer Him! Be jubilant, my feet!
   Our God is marching on.

4. In the beauty of the lilies Christ was born across the sea,
   With a glory in His bosom that transfigures you and me.
   As He died to make men holy, let us die to make men free,
   While God is marching on.

# Count Your Blessings Instead of Sheep

from the Motion Picture Irving Berlin's WHITE CHRISTMAS

**Words and Music by Irving Berlin**

# From a Distance

**Words and Music by Julie Gold**

*Additional Lyrics*

2. From a distance we all have enough, and no one is in need.
There are no guns, no bombs, no diseases, no hungry mouths to feed.
From a distance we are instruments, marching in a common band.
Playing songs of hope, playing songs of peace, they're the songs of ev'ry man.

3. From a distance you look like my friend, even though we are at war.
From a distance I can't comprehend what all this war is for.
From a distance there is harmony, and it echoes through the land.
It's the hope of hopes, it's the love of loves, it's the heart of ev'ry man.

# Give Me Your Tired, Your Poor

from the Stage Production MISS LIBERTY

**Words by Emma Lazarus**
**From the Poem "The New Colossus"**
**Music by Irving Berlin**

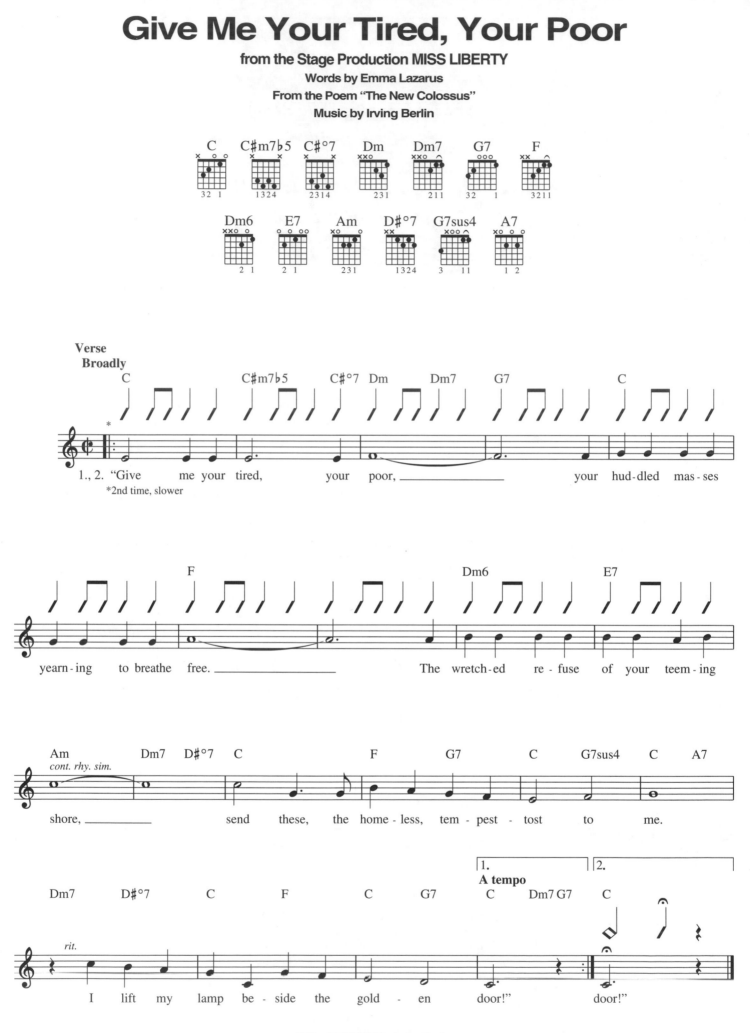

# God Bless America

**Words and Music by Irving Berlin**

11

# God Bless Our Native Land

**Traditional**

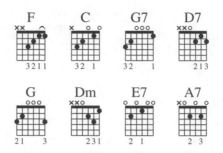

1. God bless our na-tive land, on this firm shore we
   us Thy truth and love, guide us to look a-

stand, for free - dom's rights. Let
bove, for all we need. Show

us a - rise in might, dis - pel the shades of
us the way to go, from Thee all mer - cies

night. And ban - ish them for light and
flow! Teach us Thy Name to know, and for

truth we pray. 2. Send
this we pray.

# God of Our Fathers

**Words by Daniel Crane Roberts**
**Music by George William Warren**

### Additional Lyrics

2. Thy love divine hath led us in the past,
In this free land by Thee our lot is cast.
Be Thou our ruler, guardian, guide and stay;
Thy word our law, Thy paths our chosen way.

3. From war's alarms, from deadly pestilence,
Be Thy strong arm, our ever sure defense.
Thy true religion in our hearts increase;
Thy bounteous goodness nourish us in peace.

4. Refresh Thy people on their toilsome way;
Lead us from night to neverending day.
Fill all our lives with love and grace divine,
And glory, laud, and praise be ever Thine.

# If I Had a Hammer
## (The Hammer Song)

**Words and Music by Lee Hays and Pete Seeger**

**Intro**
**Moderately fast**

1. If I ____ had a

**Verse**

ham - mer, ____ I'd a ham-mer in the morn - ing, ____

2., 3. *See additional lyrics*

____ I'd a ham-mer in the eve - ning, ____ all o - ver this

land. _____ I'd a ham-mer out dan - ger, ____ I'd a ham-mer out a

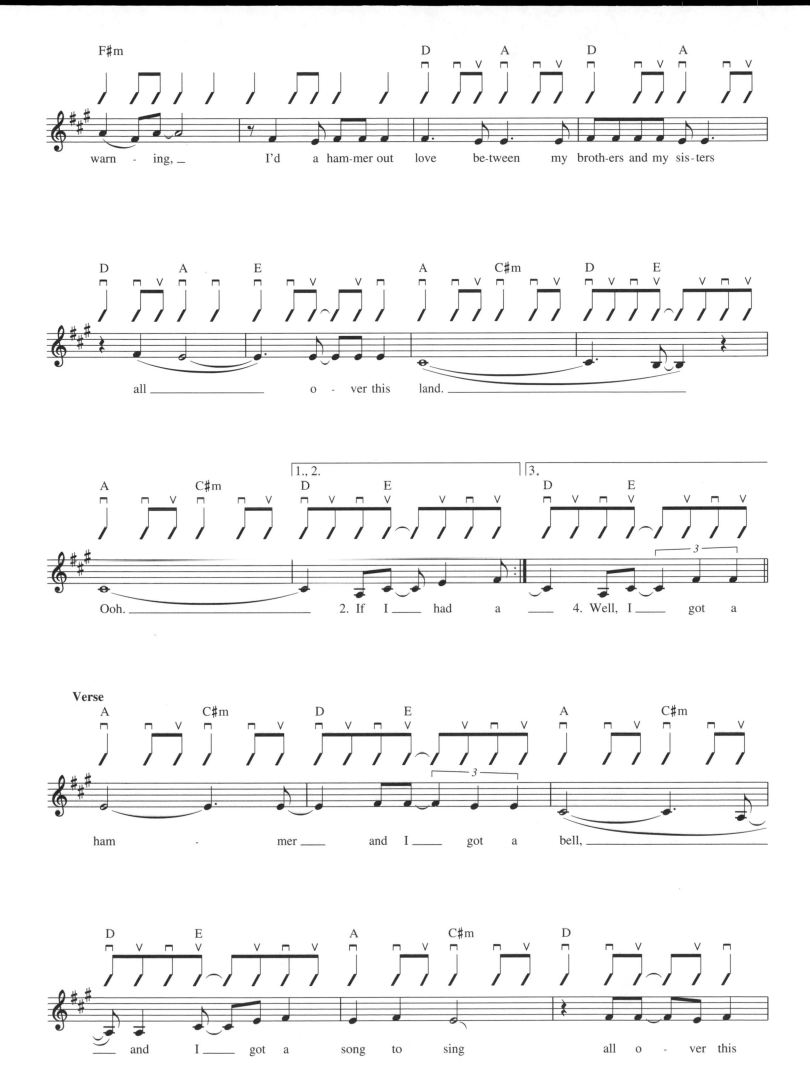

warn - ing, — I'd a ham-mer out love be-tween my broth-ers and my sis-ters

all _____ o - ver this land. _____

Ooh. _____ 2. If I ___ had a ___ 4. Well, I ___ got a

**Verse**

ham - mer ___ and I ___ got a bell, _____

___ and I ___ got a song to sing all o - ver this

## Additional Lyrics

2. If I had a bell,
   I'd a ring it in the morning,
   I'd a ring it in the evening,
   All over this land.
   I'd a ring out danger,
   I'd a ring out a warning,
   I'd a ring out love between my brothers and my sisters
   All over this land.

3. If I had a song,
   I'd sing it in the morning,
   I'd sing it in the evening,
   All over this land.
   I'd sing out danger,
   I'd sing out a warning,
   I'd sing out love between my brothers and my sisters
   All over this land.

# A Mighty Fortress Is Our God

**Words and Music by Martin Luther**
**Translated by Frederick H. Hedge**
**Based on Psalm 46**

*Additional Lyrics*

2. Did we in our own strength confide,
   Our striving would be losing;
   Were not the right man on our side,
   The man of God's own choosing;
   Dost ask who that may be?
   Christ Jesus, it is He;
   Lord Sabaoth His name,
   From age to age the same,
   And he must win the battle.

3. That word above all earthly powers,
   No thanks to them, abideth;
   The Spirit and the gifts are ours
   Through Him who with us sideth;
   Let goods and kindred go,
   This mortal life also;
   The body they may kill:
   God's truth abideth still,
   His kingdom is forever.

# Imagine

**Words and Music by John Lennon**

**Intro**
**Slowly**

**Verse**

1. Im-ag-ine there's    no heav-en.    It's eas-y    if    you ___ try. ___
2. Im-ag-ine there's    no coun-tries.    It is-n't    hard    to ___ do. ___
3. Im-ag-ine    no    po-ses-sions.    I won-der if    you ___ can. ___

___    No    hell ___    be-low us, ___
___    Noth-ing to kill ___ or die ___ for, ___
___    No need for    greed ___ or    hun-ger, ___

**Pre-Chorus**

a-bove    us on-ly sky. ___    Im-ag-ine    all ___    the ___ peo -
and no re-li-    gion ___    too. ___    Im-ag-ine    all ___    the ___ peo -
a broth-er-hood ___    of ___ man. ___    Im-ag-ine    all ___    the ___ peo -

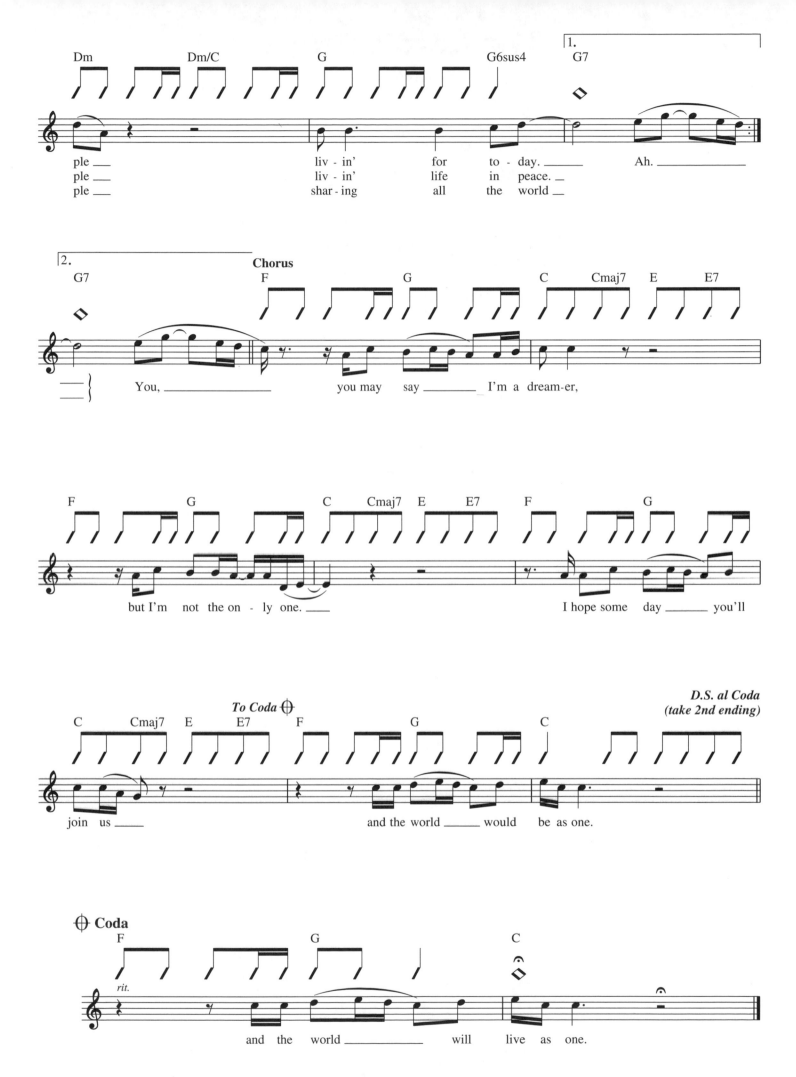

# The Lord's Prayer

By Albert Hay Malotte

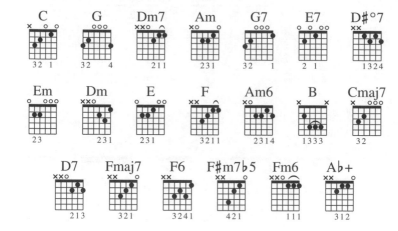

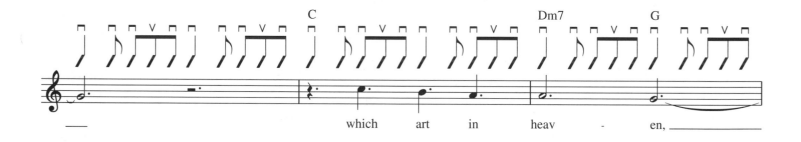

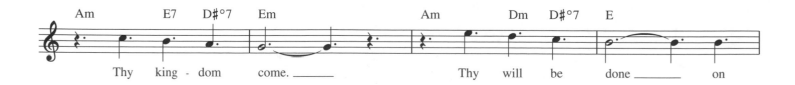

# My Country, 'Tis of Thee
## (America)

**Words by Samuel Francis Smith**
**Music from Thesaurus Musicus**

*Additional Lyrics*

3. Let music swell the breeze
And ring from all the trees
Sweet freedom's song.
Let mortal tongues awake;
Let all that breathe partake;
Let rocks their silence break,
The sound prolong.

4. Our fathers' God, to Thee
Author of liberty,
To Thee we sing.
Long may our land be bright
With freedom's holy light;
Protect us by Thy might,
Great God, our King!

# O God, Our Help in Ages Past

**Words by Isaac Watts**
**Music by William Croft**

**Verse**
**Slowly**

1. O God, our help in a - ges past, our hope for years to come, our shel - ter from the
2. *See additional lyrics*

storm - y blast, and our e - ter - nal home! Un - der the shad - ow of Thy throne, still

*cont. rhy. sim.*

may we dwell se - cure; suf - fi - cient is Thine arm a - lone, and our de - fence is

sure. Be - fore the hills in or - der stood, or earth re - ceived her frame, from

ev - er - last - ing Thou art God, to end - less years the same. 2. A home.

*Additional Lyrics*

2. A thousand age, in Thy sight, are like an evening gone;
   Short as the watch that ends the night, before the rising sun.
   Time, like an ever-rolling stream, bears all who breathe away;
   They fly forgotten, as a dream dies at the opening day.
   O God, our help in ages past, our hope for years to come.
   Be Thou our guide while life shall last, and our eternal home.

# Precious Lord, Take My Hand
## (Take My Hand, Precious Lord)

**Words and Music by Thomas A. Dorsey**

way    grows __ drear,    pre - cious Lord,    lin - ger near. ___    When my
*2. See additional lyrics*

life ___    is ___    al - most ___    gone; _____    hear my

cry,    hear my __ call, _____    hold _ my    hand    lest I    fall. ___    Take _ my

**1.**

hand, __    pre - cious    Lord, __    lead    me    home. _____    Pre - cious

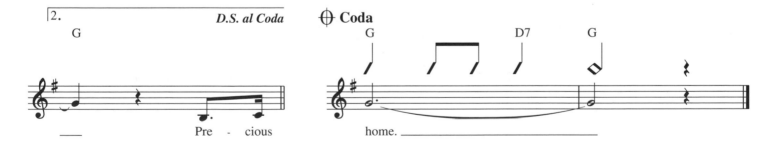

**2.**    *D.S. al Coda*    **Coda**

___    Pre - cious    home. _____

*Additional Lyrics*

2. When the darkness appears and the night draws near
   And the day is past and gone,
   At the river I stand, guide my feet, hold my hand;
   Take my hand, precious Lord, lead me home.

# The Star Spangled Banner

**Words by Francis Scott Key**
**Music by John Stafford Smith**

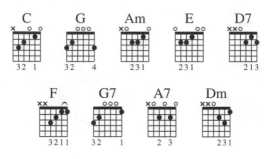

### Additional Lyrics

2. On the shore dimly seen thro' the mists of the deep,
   Where the foe's haughty host in dread silence reposes,
   What is that which the breeze, o'er the towering steep,
   As it fitfully blows, half conceals, half discloses?
   Now it catches the gleam of the morning's first beam.
   In full glory reflected now — shines in the stream.
   'Tis the star spangled banner, o long may it wave
   O'er the land of the free and the home of the brave.

3. And where is the band who so dauntingly swore,
   'Mid the havoc of war and the battle's confusion,
   A home and a country they'd leave us no more?
   Their blood has wash'd out their foul footstep's pollution.
   No refuge could save the hireling and slave
   From the terror of flight or the gloom of the grave.
   And the star spangled banner in triumph doth wave
   O'er the land of the free and the home of the brave.

4. O thus be it ever when free man shall stand,
   Between their loved homes and the war's desolation.
   Blest with the vic'try and peace, may the heav'n rescued land
   Praise the Power that hath made and preserved us a nation!
   Then conquer we must when our cause it is just,
   And this be our motto, "In God is our trust!"
   And the star spangled banner in triumph shall wave
   O'er the land of the free and the home of the brave.

# Stars and Stripes Forever

By John Philip Sousa

# This Is My Country

**Words by Don Raye**
**Music by Al Jacobs**

## Additional Lyrics

2. This is my country, land of my choice!
   This is my country; hear my proud voice!
   I pledge thee my allegiance, America the bold.
   For this is my country to have and to hold!

# This Is a Great Country

from the Stage Production MR. PRESIDENT

**Words and Music by Irving Berlin**

**Verse**
**Brightly**

Cmaj7 — C#°7 — Dm7 — G7 — C — Em6 — C#°7

Pa - tri - ot - is - m has gone out of fash - ion. _____ We seem to

Dm7 — G7 — Cmaj7 — Cmaj7 — C#°7

think our pa - tri - ot - ic days are dead. _____ We used to sing of our

Dm7  G7  C — E — F#m7 — B7
*cont. rhy. sim.*

home - land with pas - sion, _____ but now we seem to shy a - way from it in -

E — C#°7 — Dm7 — G7 — C  G9sus4  C

stead. _____ I think it's time to hit the nail right on the head. _____ This is a

# This Land Is Your Land

Words and Music by Woody Guthrie

*Symbols in parentheses represent chord names respective to capoed guitar and do not reflect actual sounding chords.

This land is

**Chorus**

your land _____ and this land is my land from Cal - i - for - nia

*Symbols in parentheses represent chord
names respective to capoed guitar. Symbols
above reflect actual sounding chords.

to the New York is - land. From the red-wood for - est to the Gulf Stream wat - ers. _____

_____ this land was made _ for you and me. 1. As I ___ went

**Verse**

walk - ing _____ that rib - bon of high - way, I saw a - bove me
ram - bled _____ and I fol-lowed my foot - steps through the spar - kling sands of
3., 4. *See additional lyrics*

*Additional Lyrics*

3., 4. When the sun comes shining as I was strolling,
The wheat fields waving and the dust clouds rolling,
A voice come a-chanting as the fog was lifting,
"This land was made for you and me."

# United We Stand

**Words and Music by Anthony Toby Hiller and John Goodison**

# We Shall Overcome

**Musical and Lyrical Adaptation by Zilphia Horton, Frank Hamilton, Guy Carawan and Pete Seeger**
**Inspired by African American Gospel Singing,**
members of the Food and Tobacco Workers Union, Charleston, SC, and the southern Civil Rights Movement

# You'll Never Walk Alone

## from CAROUSEL

**Lyrics by Oscar Hammerstein II**
**Music by Richard Rodgers**

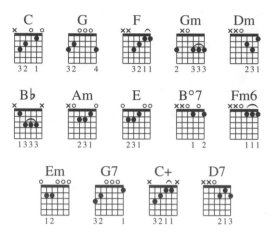

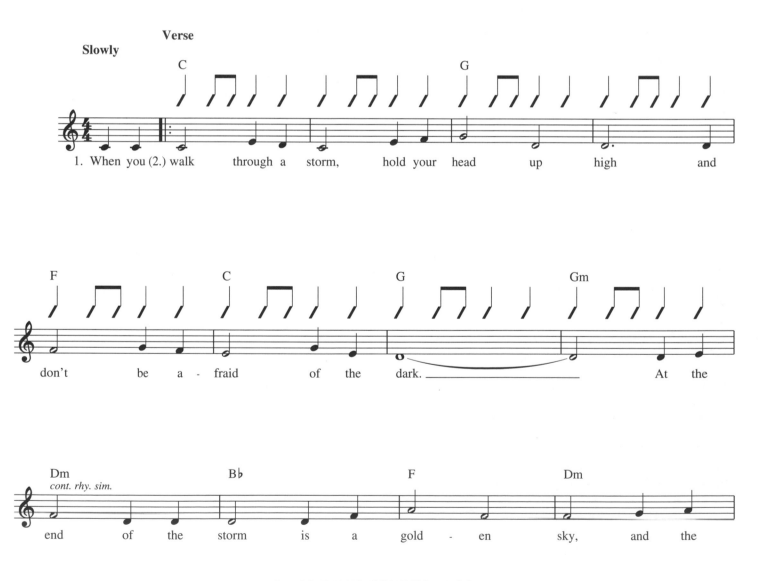

1. When you (2.) walk through a storm, hold your head up high and

don't be a - fraid of the dark. _____ At the

end of the storm is a gold - en sky, and the

# You're a Grand Old Flag

### from GEORGE M!

**Words and Music by George M. Cohan**

# STRUM IT GUITAR

**• AUTHENTIC CHORDS • ORIGINAL KEYS • COMPLETE SONGS •**

The *Strum It* series lets players strum the chords and sing along with their favorite hits. Each song has been selected because it can be played with regular open chords, barre chords, or other moveable chord types. Guitarists can simply play the rhythm, or play and sing along through the entire song. All songs are shown in their original keys complete with chords, strum patterns, melody and lyrics. Wherever possible, the chord voicings from the recorded versions are notated.

## Acoustic Classics

Play along with the recordings of 21 acoustic classics. Songs include: And I Love Her • Angie • Barely Breathing • Free Fallin' • Maggie May • Melissa • Mr. Jones • Only Wanna Be with You • Patience • Signs • Teach Your Children • Wonderful Tonight • Wonderwall • Yesterday • and more.
00699238 $9.95

## The Beatles Favorites

Features 23 classic Beatles hits, including: Can't Buy Me Love • Eight Days a Week • Hey Jude • I Saw Her Standing There • Let It Be • Nowhere Man • She Loves You • Something • Yesterday • You've Got to Hide Your Love Away • and more.
00699249 $10.95

## Celtic Guitar Songbook

Features 35 complete songs in their original keys, with authentic chords, strum patterns, melody and lyrics. Includes: Black Velvet Band • Cockles and Mussels (Molly Malone) • Danny Boy (Londonderry Air) • Finnegan's Wake • Galway Bay • I'm a Rover and Seldom Sober • The Irish Washerwoman • Kerry Dance • Killarncy • McNamara's Band • My Wild Irish Rose • The Rose of Tralee • Sailor's Hornpipe • Whiskey in the Jar • Wild Rover • and more.
00699265 $9.95

## Christmas Songs for Guitar

Over 40 Christmas favorites, including: The Christmas Song (Chestnuts Roasting on an Open Fire) • Feliz Navidad • Frosty the Snow Man • Grandma Got Run Over by a Reindeer • The Greatest Gift of All • I'll Be Home for Christmas • It's Beginning to Look Like Christmas • Rockin' Around the Christmas Tree • Silver Bells • and more.
00699247 $9.95

## Country Strummin'

Features 24 songs: Achy Breaky Heart • Adalida • Ain't That Lonely Yet • Blue • The Beaches of Cheyenne • A Broken Wing • Gone Country • I Fall to Pieces • My Next Broken Heart • She and I • Unchained Melody • What a Crying Shame • and more.
00699119 $8.95

## Jim Croce – Classic Hits

Authentic chords to 22 great songs from Jim Croce, including: Bad, Bad Leroy Brown • I'll Have to Say I Love You in a Song • Operator (That's Not the Way It Feels) • Time in a Bottle • and more.
00699269 $10.95

## Disney Favorites

A great collection of 34 easy-to-play Disney favorites. Includes: Can You Feel the Love Tonight • Circle of Life • Cruella De Vil • Friend Like Me • It's a Small World • Some Day My Prince Will Come • Under the Sea • Whistle While You Work • Winnie the Pooh • Zero to Hero • and more.
00699171 $10.95

## Disney Greats

Easy arrangements with guitar chord frames and strum patterns for 39 wonderful Disney classics including: Arabian Nights • The Aristocats • Beauty and the Beast • Colors of the Wind • Go the Distance • Hakuna Matata • Heigh-Ho • Kiss the Girl • A Pirate's Life • When You Wish Upon a Star • Zip-A-Dee-Doo-Dah • Theme from Zorro • and more.
00699172 $10.95

## The Doors

Strum along with more than 25 of your favorite hits from The Doors. Includes: Been Down So Long • Hello I Love You Won't You Tell Me Your Name? • Light My Fire • Riders on the Storm • Touch Me • and more.
00699177 $10.95

## Favorite Songs With 3 Chords

27 popular songs that are easy to play, including: All Shook Up • Blue Suede Shoes • Boot Scootin' Boogie • Evil Ways • Great Balls of Fire • Lay Down Sally • Semi-Charmed Life • Surfin' U.S.A. • Twist and Shout • Wooly Bully • and more.
00699112 $8.95

## Great '50s Rock

28 of early rock's biggest hits, including: At the Hop • Blueberry Hill • Bye Bye Love • Hound Dog • Rock Around the Clock • That'll Be the Day • and more.
00699187 $8.95

## Great '60s Rock

Features the chords, strum patterns, melody and lyrics for 27 classic rock songs, all in their original keys. Includes: And I Love Her • Crying • Gloria • Good Lovin' • I Fought the Law • Mellow Yellow • Return to Sender • Runaway • Surfin' U.S.A. • The Twist • Twist and Shout • Under the Boardwalk • Wild Thing • and more.
00699188 $8.95

## Great '70s Rock

Strum the chords to 21 classic '70s hits! Includes: Band on the Run • Burning Love • If • It's a Heartache • Lay Down Sally • Let It Be • Love Hurts • Maggie May • New Kid in Town • Ramblin' Man • Time for Me to Fly • Two Out of Three Ain't Bad • Wild World • and more.
00699262 $8.95

## Great '80s Rock

23 arrangements that let you play along with your favorite recordings from the 1980s, such as: Back on the Chain Gang • Centerfold • Crazy Little Thing Called Love • Free Fallin' • Got My Mind Set on You • Kokomo • Should I Stay or Should I Go • Uptown Girl • Waiting for a Girl Like You • What I Like About You • and more.
00699263 $8.95

## Hymn Favorites

Includes: Amazing Grace • Battle Hymn of the Republic • Blessed Assurance • Down by the Riverside • Holy, Holy, Holy • In the Garden • Just as I Am • O Worship the King • Rock of Ages • This Is My Father's World • Wayfaring Stranger • What a Friend We Have in Jesus • and more.
00699271 $9.95

## Best of Sarah McLachlan

20 of Sarah's most popular hits for guitar, including: Adia • Angel • Building a Mystery • I Will Remember You • Ice Cream • Sweet Surrender • and more.
00699231 $10.95

## A Merry Christmas Songbook

Easy arrangements for 51 holiday hits: Away in a Manger • Deck the Hall • Fum, Fum, Fum • The Holly and the Ivy • Jolly Old St. Nicholas • O Christmas Tree • Star of the East • The Twelve Days of Christmas • more!
00699211 $8.95

## Pop-Rock Guitar Favorites

31 songs, including: Angie • Brown Eyed Girl • Crazy Little Thing Called Love • Eight Days a Week • Fire and Rain • Free Bird • Gloria • Hey Jude • Let It Be • Maggie May • New Kid in Town • Surfin' U.S.A. • Wild Thing • Wonderful Tonight • and more.
00699088 $8.95

## Best of George Strait

Strum the chords to 20 great Strait hits! Includes: Adalida • All My Ex's Live in Texas • The Best Day • Blue Clear Sky • Carried Away • The Chair • Does Fort Worth Ever Cross Your Mind • Lovebug • Right or Wrong • Write This Down • and more.
00699235 $10.95

## Best of Hank Williams Jr.

24 of Hank's signature standards. Includes: Ain't Misbehavin' • All My Rowdy Friends Are Coming Over Tonight • Attitude Adjustment • Family Tradition • Honky Tonkin' • Texas Women • There's a Tear in My Beer • Whiskey Bent and Hell Bound • and more.
00699224 $10.95

## Women of Rock

22 hits from today's top female artists. Includes: Bitch • Don't Speak • Galileo • Give Me One Reason • I Don't Want to Wait • Insensitive • Lovefool • Mother Mother • Stay • Torn • You Oughta Know • You Were Meant for Me • Zombie • and more.
00699183 $9.95